P9-EBY-366

T

NATURE'S MYSTERIES

HOW INSECTS WORK TOGETHER

Jill Bailey

BENCHMARK BOOKS

MARSHALL CAVENDISH
NEW YORK

Benchmark Books
Marshall Cavendish Corporation
99 White Plains Road
Tarrytown, New York 10591-9001

©Marshall Cavendish Corporation, 1999

Series created by Discovery Books

Library of Congress Cataloging-in-Publication Data
Bailey, Jill
     How insects work together/Jill Bailey
     p. cm. - (Nature's Mysteries)
     Includes bibliographical references and index.
     Summary: Examines the lives and survival techniques of social insects, who live together in colonies where different members of the group perform different tasks, including termites, wasps, ants, and honeybees.
     ISBN 0-7614-0859-2
     1. Insect societies - Juvenile literature. [1. Insect societies. 2. Insects.] I. Title. II. Series.
     QL496.B338 1998   98-22669 CIP AC
     595.7156-DC21

Printed in Hong Kong

Acknowledgments
Text consultant: Phil Pellitteri, Insect Diagnostic Lab, University of Wisconsin/Madison.
Illustrated by Stuart Lafford
The publishers would like to thank the following for their permission to reproduce
photographs: cover K.G Preston-Mafham/Premaphotos Wildlife, title page K.G Preston-Mafham/Premaphotos Wildlife, 4 David Thompson/Oxford Scientific Films, 5 Harald Lange/Bruce Coleman, 6 top K.G Preston-Mafham/Premaphotos Wildlife, 7 Kim Taylor/Bruce Coleman, 8 Konrad Wothe/Oxford Scientific Films, 9 K.G Preston-Mafham/Premaphotos Wildlife, 10 Aldo Brando/Oxford Scientific Films, 11 bottom Dr. Sandro Prato/Bruce Coleman, 11 top B. Borrell/FLPA, 12 Alan Root/Survival Anglia/Oxford Scientific Films, 13 Petr Zabransky/Bruce Coleman, 15 bottom K.G Preston-Mafham/Premaphotos Wildlife, 15 top Philip Sharpe/Oxford Scientific Films, 17 top K.G Preston-Mafham/Premaphotos Wildlife, 17 bottom T. Davidson/FLPA, 18 & 19 top Kim Taylor/Bruce Coleman, 20 top & bottom K.G Preston-Mafham/Premaphotos Wildlife, 21 Mantis Wildlife Films/Oxford Scientific Films, 22 K.G Preston-Mafham/Premaphotos Wildlife, 23 top G.I. Bernard/Oxford Scientific Films, 23 bottom K.G Preston-Mafham/Premaphotos Wildlife, 24 Derek Bromhall/Oxford Scientific Films, 25 K.G Preston-Mafham/Premaphotos Wildlife, 26 top Alan Root/Survival Anglia/Oxford Scientific Films, 28 K.G Preston-Mafham/Premaphotos Wildlife, 29 Neil Bromhall/Oxford Scientific Films.

(Cover) Leaf-cutter ants carrying a leaf back to their nest.

CONTENTS

You may often have watched ants as they scurry across the ground or honeybees buzzing in and out of flowers. You probably know that they are collecting food. What is less obvious, however, is that these ants and bees are part of a team. Each insect is performing a specific and vital task that is essential to the whole community. Contributing to the community is what it means to be a social insect.

Social insects live in large groups called colonies, where different members of the group perform different tasks. Social insects cannot survive by themselves. Their existence depends on working with each other

A social insect colony is usually ruled by one female, the queen, who lays all the eggs. The queen, as well as the eggs, the young, and the nest, are cared for by a team of workers. You can see this honeybee queen being groomed by the smaller workers around her.

to keep the colony going. All ants and termites, and some species of bees and wasps, are social insects.

Why be social? With large numbers working together, all members of the group have a better chance of survival than solitary insects. Several generations live in the same nest, care for the young, gather food, and maintain and defend the nest. Some insects can stay behind as guards while others forage outside. Some can look after the young while others are cleaning and repairing the nest.

The world population of social insects is astounding. A single ant is only one-millionth the weight of a human, yet the combined weight of all the world's ants matches that of all humans! A honeybee colony may contain up to 80,000 bees, while termites live in groups of over one million. These numbers are evidence of a very successful way of life. We're going to look at the ways in which social insects work together to survive.

This termitarium, home to many thousands of termites, has been built by teamwork. It contains an intricate network of chambers and air vents, both above and below the ground.

A lthough social insects appear to live quite complicated lives, they are not really very intelligent. So how do they manage to work together so efficiently?

Bees and wasps have good color vision for finding food while in flight. But inside their nests it is dark, so they must use other senses. All social insects rely heavily on touch and smell, both for finding their way and for communicating with each other. Their behavior is made up of a series of automatic responses to particular signals. For instance, the smell of a hungry youngster causes an adult to bring food. Ants and termites have poor sight or none at all, but they respond to sounds and other vibrations.

A newly emerged termite queen tries to attract a male by flapping her wings, raising her abdomen and releasing a special pheromone.

Social insects use many different chemicals to send specific messages to each other. These chemicals are called pheromones. Some act as a kind of personal identification card. Each social insect bears the scent of its

Social insects often use postures and gestures for communicating. This tropical ant queen (left) has challenged another ant (right) by lunging at her with open jaws. Her opponent signals that she doesn't want to take up the challenge and fight by flattening herself against the ground.

colony, which is different from that of other colonies. An insect's scent tells other insects who it is and can reveal its sex, status, and age.

This smell, which to our noses might resemble a rather smelly gas station, comes from several sources. The nest itself has a distinctive smell, and the workers may also produce their own inherited scents. Scents are also passed around the colony by workers as they groom and feed each other. The queens of many species produce the most powerful pheromones of all. These chemicals appear to keep the workers calm and contented and also prevent them from breeding.

Alarm pheromones are produced when an insect is disturbed. These cause its coworkers to become very alert. Some may respond by rushing back to the nest to recruit more workers to defend the colony.

Away from the nest, ants and termites also lay chemical trails when they are out foraging, touching their abdomens to the ground as they go. These tell other workers where they have found food.

A honeybee worker that has found a good source of food performs a special dance on the comb when she returns. The pattern of her dance tells the other bees the direction and distance of the new food source. Her smell tells them about the kind of food she has found.

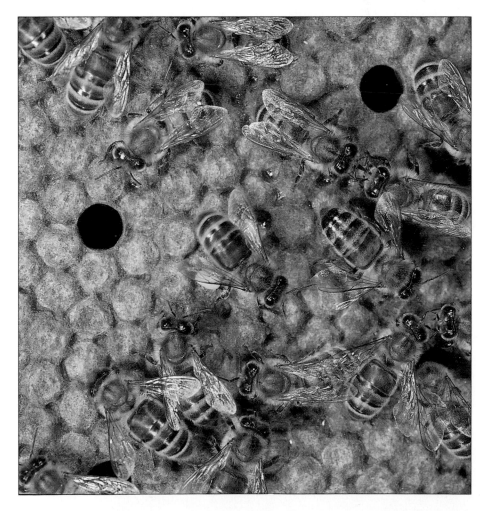

THE PECKING ORDER

Social insect colonies have a strict caste system. This means that some individuals in the same species are different in size from others and play a different role in the colony.

The honeybee queen, for example, is much larger than the other bees in her colony. Her job is simply to lay eggs. The males, known as drones, are smaller and also have only one job: to mate with the queen. Smaller still are the workers, the females who do all the work in the hive.

All the castes are of course necessary to survival, but it is the worker castes that are the mainstay of all social

Worker castes come in many different sizes. The soldier of the leaf-cutter ant is 300 times bigger than the smallest worker caste, with several different sized workers in between. Here, two minor workers are riding on a leaf carried by a major worker. The minors' role is to fend off tiny wasps that might try to attack the major worker.

insect colonies. They have a variety of work to do. In wasp colonies, all the workers tend to share all the tasks. Honeybees, ants, and termites, however, have their own special duties depending on their age and size.

What makes an insect turn into a particular caste? The caste of ants, bees, and wasps is determined by a mixture of inheritance and feeding. The males come from unfertilized eggs, while the workers (all female) come from fertilized eggs. The worker caste in an ant colony seems to be decided by the size of egg laid and the nature of the food it gets as a larva. Female bee larvae that are fed exclusively on a food called royal jelly develop into queens.

Some ants and termites have a caste of workers known as soldiers. This column of African driver ants is guarded by the much larger soldiers.

Termite colonies are different from those of other social insects because they contain nearly equal numbers of male and female workers. All termite castes come from fertilized eggs, and workers may be male or female. The male workers are sometimes larger than females and do heavier tasks.

At any stage of its growth, a termite may change into a soldier or a breeding caste. Usually this is prevented by chemicals produced by the king and queen. These either suppress the change, or cause the other workers to destroy any termites that start to change caste. When more queens, kings or soldiers are needed, the royal pair reduce the chemical output allowing the change to proceed.

THE BABYSITTERS

Bees, wasps, and ants all develop from an egg into a larva, which just feeds and molts from time to time as it grows bigger. Eventually it stops feeding and becomes a pupa, an inactive stage during which the insect is turning into an adult. This process is called metamorphosis. Young insects at all stages of development are cared for by workers until they are old enough to look after themselves. The underground nest of a meadow ant has many chambers devoted to rearing the young. When eggs are laid by the queen, nursery workers carry them to one of these chambers, where they keep them clean and moist by licking them.

When the eggs hatch into larvae, the workers tirelessly tend to their charges, feeding and cleaning them constantly. Developing pupae are carried by the nursery workers closer to the ground surface, where they will be warmed by the sun. This speeds up their change into adult ants.

Ants use their jaws to carry eggs and young from place to place. Although their jaws have sharp cutting edges, the ants manage to carry the larvae and pupae without harming them.

At night, when it gets cooler, workers carry larvae and pupae deeper into the nest for warmth.

These paper wasp nurses are tending larvae in their cells. As well as feeding them, the workers must lick the larvae to keep them clean, so they are not infected by germs or fungi. The sealed cells you can see contain pupae at various stages.

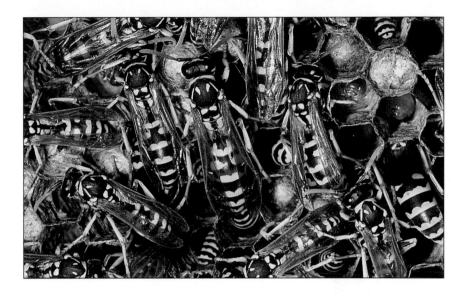

The cells at the center of the honeybee's comb are kept as brood cells for eggs and larvae. The queen lays a single egg in each cell. When the egg hatches into a larva, the young honeybees on nursery duty start to care for them. They feed them on demand, responding to signals from the growing larvae. When a larva has grown to fill its cell, the nurse bees seal it in with a layer of wax to pupate. After about twelve days, the new bee cuts its way out with the help of its nurses.

Termites don't pupate. Instead of the big change in shape and size (metamorphosis) that bees and ants have, termites change gradually, shedding their skins from time to time as they grow. Because they change gradually, their young are called nymphs instead of larvae. They are cared for by nursery workers until they have shed their first skin. They carry out different duties as they grow bigger. Young adults usually care for the eggs and nymphs in special nursery chambers. The older adults go out to forage.

Pupae of honeybee drones inside their sealed cells.

THE ROYAL ROLE

As we have discovered, the job of the social insect queen is to lay eggs. The other insects in her colony relieve her of other tasks. Not only do they feed her young, build, repair, and clean the nest, but they also feed and groom the queen herself, and defend her from danger. Because she can devote all her energies to laying eggs, a single queen can produce millions of eggs in her lifetime.

Some queens start out by doing other jobs. Until their first batch of workers are grown, bumblebee, ant, and termite queens will look after the nest and eggs. But when the first workers are ready to forage for food, the queen gives up any work other than laying eggs.

Queens can grow to a huge size. Termite queens, with their swollen abdomens, are many times bigger than their workers and incapable of doing anything for themselves. Queens of all species are usually surrounded by workers performing their grooming and feeding duties.

In the heart of the termite's mound is a royal chamber, where the huge termite queen and her king lie, surrounded by attentive workers. The king is the larger termite in the center foreground.

Termites are the only social insects in which the king (equivalent to the drone) has a long life after the mating flight. After meeting on the mating flight, the royal pair make an underground chamber in which they will mate and start their nest. Among the other social insects, the male dies

A honeybee swarm is made up of thousands of workers surrounding the old queen. She has left the nest in the control of a new queen and will now start a new colony.

after mating with the queen. The newly mated queen is able to store the male's sperm for many years and use it to fertilize her eggs as she lays them.

BUILDING THE NEST

One of the most amazing tasks performed by social insects is the building of their nests. These complicated structures take several different forms, and most require that the insects work as a team.

Let's look first at an ants' nest. When the first batch of workers has been raised, they soon begin nest building in earnest. Starting from the small underground chamber already made by the queen, the workers begin to dig tunnels. They dig with their front claws and jaws and then carry the soil, piece by piece, up to the surface.

Some tropical ants, who live in colonies containing up to eighty million workers, dig out forty-four tons of soil while excavating a nest. This is about a billion ant-loads, each weighing five times the weight of the worker ant carrying it.

Inside their nest, ants construct an elaborate network of tunnels and chambers. The chambers are positioned to suit their purposes. Deep in the ground, and less vulnerable to freezing, are chambers used in winter. Nursery workers are constantly moving eggs and pupae from one part of the nest to another as temperatures change (1). Safe in the middle are the queen's chambers (2) and maybe storage rooms for food. Here, nursery workers tend the newly-laid eggs (3). Dotted about the nest are workers' resting places and nursery chambers for larvae in various stages of development.

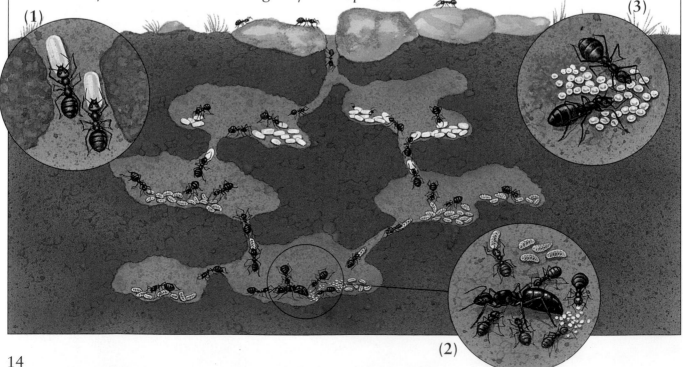

Excavated soil may pile up to form a mound called an anthill, which also becomes part of the nest. Red wood ants often build their homes around tree stumps, with the nest extending above and below the ground. The chambers above the ground are added to with plant material and twigs, covered by a layer of pine needles. Thousands of pieces of building material are collected and brought to the nest. Teams of ants handle the heavier pieces together.

Not all ants live on the ground or under it. Weaver ants and tailor ants build leafy nests high in the trees. The weaver ants pull leaves together by forming living chains of ants, hanging

Army ants and driver ants make temporary living nests called bivouacs. Hundreds of thousands of ants link themselves together by gripping each other with their claws. The queen and the young are well protected in the middle of the seething ball of ants.

onto each other's waists with their claws, until one leaf is pulled down onto another. Other workers will pick up ant larvae and bring them to the leaf edges. When they tap the larvae with their feelers, the larvae produce silk to stick the leaves together.

Weaver ants work as a team to pull leaves into place to build their nest. Their larvae will stick the leaves together with silk.

15

Termites live in a variety of nests and often make their own building materials. Some termites mix their saliva with chewed-up wood to form a paste. They use the mixture the way a bricklayer uses bricks, adding small lumps to build walls and tunnels.

Chimneys to draw air through nest

Mound of soil mixed with saliva

Fungus gardens

Ground water *(moistens air for fungus to grow)*

Royal chamber

Nursery chambers

Air cellar *(draws in air from soil)*

The paste dries to make a firm, cardboard-like nest, which may hang from a branch or be built into the ground.

Termite mounds are among the largest structures made by animals. Some tower into the sky and can be seen for miles around. They may extend several feet below ground, too. In Africa, termite workers make their mounds by extracting grains of sand from the subsoil and bringing them to the surface. Working together in vast numbers and at incredible speed, they cement the sand with their saliva and excrement, building mounds many feet high and nearly as hard as rocks when they dry.

Social bees and wasps build nests of a different kind. They construct cells, which are little individual

The tall towers on the mound are part of the termites' remarkable air-conditioning system. Fresh air and constant temperatures are maintained inside the nest by a series of passages and vents. Inside, workers are busy opening some vents and blocking off others to help regulate the airflow.

Paper wasps chew tiny strips of wood, mixing them with their saliva to make a pulp that dries into paper. At first this job is done by a single female (the queen), but when she has raised her first team of workers, they take over the job of enlarging the nest cell by cell.

and mouth to shape a small lump of pulp into the walls of a cell.

Bees use wax produced by their own glands to build their cells. When young honeybee workers develop these glands, they start constructing cells at the edge of the existing comb. They grip slivers of wax in their jaws and mold them into perfcct, six-sided shapes with their mouths.

chambers made to hold eggs, developing young, and food supplies. The cells are all joined together to form a layer called a comb. Some nests may have just a few cells in one comb, but others have many combs and thousands of cells.

Wasps make cells from chewed-up wood or other plant fibers, which they shape into cells, building each one onto the last. To do this, they use their legs

Hundreds of bees work together to build the comb in a honeybee nest. To help each other reach difficult spots, the bees form a chain with their bodies.

GOOD HOUSEKEEPING

After they have made their nests, social insects devote a great deal of time to maintaining, repairing, and cleaning their homes. Often the tasks carried out by a worker depend upon its age. A young worker honeybee, for example, cleans the hive. Later, when special glands in her head are mature, she produces royal jelly and other food to feed the larvae. Then these glands shrink and her wax glands are ready for nest building. She will also make honey now. Only the oldest and largest workers go out to forage. This is very dangerous work, and the colony has already got a lot out of these workers. If they are killed at this time, their lives will not have been wasted.

Ants are also constantly busy with cleaning duties. They remove anything that may cause rot or mildew in the nest.

Some ants have a special chamber for garbage, and others carry it out of the nest altogether.

Social insects have different ways of cooling and airing their nests. Chains of ants bring water into the nest by passing it to each other, like people passing buckets at a fire. Other ants inside the nest spread the water on the walls and floor to evaporate.

Honeybee workers fanning at the hive entrance to waft warm air out and let cooler air in. The sound of hundreds of bees fanning together on the edge of their nest is similar to hot water bubbling on a stove.

Honeybees control the temperature of their nest by fanning their wings to cool it down. If it gets very hot, some workers leave the nest to bring back water. They pass it to other workers who act as reservoirs for the whole nest. They spread it over their brood cells or stick out their wet tongues, so the water on them evaporates and cools the air.

If a nest is damaged by an enemy or by the weather, workers immediately rush to repair it. This is an instinctive process, a response to the sight or feel of the damage. Even workers engaged in other tasks may stop and join the repair crew until the emergency has passed.

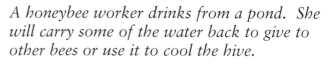

A honeybee worker drinks from a pond. She will carry some of the water back to give to other bees or use it to cool the hive.

A few ant species have found an easy way of dealing with the endless housework. They actually make slaves of other species! Samurai ants in Japan, for example, raid black ant colonies and steal their larvae and pupae. The black ants are then raised to do the work of the Samurai colony. They feed, forage, and take care of the nest.

Amazon ants make a raid on another ants' nest to capture slaves. Amazon ants are so dependent on their slaves that they cannot forage or raise their own young.

19

In social insect colonies, even eating is a communal task. Workers are responsible for the important task of feeding their queen and larvae, but they also have some ingenious methods of feeding their coworkers.

Most social insects feed each other by passing liquid food from mouth to mouth. In ant colonies, it is the job of the food-gathering ants to feed others. The ant eats some of the food it collects but stores most of it in its community stomach, or crop, to be shared with others. When another ant wants some food, it uses its antennae to stroke the head of the food gatherer, who then feeds it.

Two tropical ants exchange liquid food mouth-to-mouth. In this way chemicals that convey the colony smell are passed around.

Honeybees can obtain nectar from foraging bees in a similar way. Worker bees inside the hive may eat some of the nectar, but they will also feed it to drones and the queen or turn it into honey to be stored in cells.

Feeding the larvae requires a special workforce. Honeybee nursery workers produce a rich substance, known as royal jelly, to feed larvae for the first few days. Worker larvae are fed on royal jelly for the first three days of their lives, queen larvae for the whole period of their development.

A social wasp offers a ball of food which it has regurgitated to a larva in its cell.

Worker wasps chew their insect prey to a pulp to feed to their larvae. A paper wasp will bang her head on a larva's cell and buzz to let it know the food has arrived. The larva then adopts a certain position to persuade the worker to give up the food.

Many social insect queens are as incapable as the larvae of finding food or feeding themselves. Termites feed their queen with their own food. In turn, her attendant workers can feed on the drops of sweet liquid the queen excretes. A honeybee queen is fed mouth-to-mouth by her attendants on a liquid of partly digested nectar and pollen, while ant queens receive ground-up insects or seeds.

Storing food for future use is yet another task in the social insect colony. Honeybees build up a good cache of honey in cells to see them through the winter, when there will be no foraging outside the hive. Similarly, harvester ants build chambers to store seeds for times when food is scarce.

Some Californian honey ants act as storage pots for the rest of their colony. The workers who perform this noble task are known as repletes. Their huge bellies are swollen with honeydew, a sugary liquid produced by aphids. Repletes are so valuable that they are sometimes stolen by other colonies.

HUNTERS AND GATHERERS

Foraging for food or hunting for prey is the most dangerous task for a worker. Usually only the older workers forage, after they have already contributed a useful life to the colony. For every twelve harvester ants out foraging for seeds, at least one dies in fights with its neighbors, and some are also killed by predators.

Ants of some species first send out scouts to hunt for food. If the scouts find a large insect, they go back to the nest for help. By tapping other workers with their antennae, the scouts get the reinforcements they need to bring the food back to the nest. Some forager ants and termites lay scent trails for other members of their colony. They release chemicals from their abdomens along the route, and soon a whole team of workers will be scurrying back and forth between the food source and the nest.

Many ants are hunters. They kill or paralyze other insects with poisoned bites or spray. Working as a team, ants can overwhelm prey much larger than themselves by sheer force of numbers. These driver ants from the Kakamega forest in Kenya are attacking and killing an assassin bug.

Termites prefer to forage for their food under cover. Many species live on a diet of wood, and their foragers will leave the nest through a network of underground tunnels to reach a food source such as fallen trees or branches. If they absolutely must go above ground, some termites construct covered runways from soil or wood pulp. These run from their nest to favorite foraging grounds, going across the ground and even up trees and buildings!

▲ *A bumblebee worker gets covered in pollen as she laps up nectar from a flower. She will store the nectar in her crop to take it back to the nest. She will scrape the pollen into special baskets on her legs for the flight home.*

▼ *A column of foraging termites follows a scent trail to and from the nest.*

Honeybees and wasps cannot lay scent trails on the ground, as they forage from the air. They may chew up food or suck up nectar and swallow it, storing it in their stomachs until they get back to the nest. Pollen sticks to the bodies of bees while they are foraging for nectar. They scrape it off into special baskets of bristles on their legs.

THE FARMERS

Some social insects use farming methods to obtain their food! Leaf-cutter ants live on a kind of fungus that they cultivate in underground chambers. They grow the fungus on fragments of leaves.

This crop-raising job requires the efforts of the whole team. Leaf-cutter ants have several worker castes of varying sizes. Large foragers, guarded by even bigger soldiers, cut and bring back sections of leaves. Smaller workers chop the leaves into tiny pieces, and even smaller ones chew them up and add them to the compost in the fungus garden.

The smallest ants tend the crop. Tiny workers plant scraps of fungus in the new compost. The smallest caste of all can squeeze between the fungus threads to lick them clean and do the weeding.

Leaf-cutter ants at work in their fungus garden deep inside the nest. They are chewing leaves and weeding out other fungi.

Red ants look after a herd of bean aphids. The ants move the herd around in search of new plants for the aphids to feed on.

Many termites also cultivate fungus in special chambers or gardens. The fungus grows on partly chewed wood and plant fibers brought into the nest by foragers. The fungus breaks down the food into a softer form that the termites like to eat. The growing fungus and rotting plant material give off lots of heat, which is swept away by the air-conditioning.

Some ants practice a form of farming that is somewhat like dairy farming, in which cows are kept for milk. These ants keep aphids and other insects in shelters, protecting them from predators and keeping them clean.

The farmed insects can then provide the ants with food, in the form of honeydew. This is the sweet liquid they excrete after eating the sap from plants. The ants "milk" the aphids by tapping them with their antennae, causing them to relase drops of honeydew.

DEFENSE AND ATTACK

The social insects face enemies on all sides. Apart from birds, spiders, anteaters, badgers, and a host of other furred and feathered enemies, they are attacked by other insects— especially by other social insects.

Guarding the colony is vital to all social insects. Worker honeybees take their turn for guard duty when they reach a certain age. Ants and termites often rely on their soldier castes to guard them.

The smell of a foreign insect will provoke a guard to attack, regardless of what the intruder looks like or how big it is. Most social insects, of any caste, have an armory of chemical

▲ *Anteaters have powerful curved claws for tearing into the nest and a long, sticky tongue for licking up prey.*

◄ *Some ants use gestures to try to avoid fighting. These pairs of ants are from neighboring colonies that compete with each other for food. At favorite display grounds they are trying to look as fierce as possible, standing on tiptoe and spreading their jaws wide to try to persuade the neighbors that they are a force to be reckoned with. The display ends when one side retreats. If the display is not good enough, the neighbors may attack anyway.*

weapons in their bites and stings. The soldier castes of ants and termites use their powerful jaws to nip off the limbs and heads of their enemies. Others squirt poison, or even glue. If all defenses fail, some workers may flee with the queen, eggs, larvae, and pupae while the soldiers stay and fight to the death.

Rival ant colonies often attack each other to gain territory or steal food. Repletes, with their store of honeydew, may be stolen by neighboring colonies in fierce raids. Robber ants will make forays to steal the pupae of other ant species. Some will be eaten and others raised as slaves.

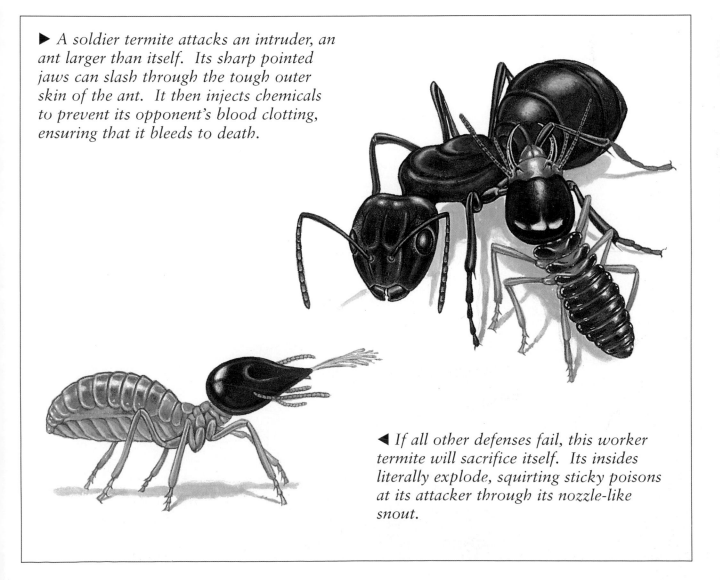

▶ A soldier termite attacks an intruder, an ant larger than itself. Its sharp pointed jaws can slash through the tough outer skin of the ant. It then injects chemicals to prevent its opponent's blood clotting, ensuring that it bleeds to death.

◀ If all other defenses fail, this worker termite will sacrifice itself. Its insides literally explode, squirting sticky poisons at its attacker through its nozzle-like snout.

It is not only insects that work together to survive. Some of the most unexpected animals have organized social lives.

In the tropics huge communal spider webs are common, some of them many feet high. These large webs catch flying insects bigger than those a single spider could deal with. As soon as something lands in the web, several spiders rush to subdue it. The larger the insect, the bigger its vibrations, and the more spiders come to attack it. Working together and sharing food means that spiders need to tell their prey from their web-mates. They do this by detecting the different vibrations made on the web by fellow spiders and struggling captives.

The strangest social animals are tiny mites that live in the ears of moths.

Social spiders in the Amazon rain forest make a joint attack on a dragonfly.

Here, several females dig out a chamber and work together to rear their young. There are special areas for eggs, young, mating, molting, and waste. Even if the nest gets crowded, they never take over the moth's other ear. This ensures that the moth can hear the approach of bats and other enemies, and so survive.

Many large animals live in groups or herds and help each other survive. But the naked molerats of Africa are the only large animals that, like social

Naked molerats have a social structure that is similar to that of social insects. It may be that the breeding female produces a pheromone that prevents the others from breeding.

insects, have breeders and workers. Molerat colonies live in underground burrow systems, just like many ants and termites. Only one pair of molerats breeds, and the rest act like workers, feeding the breeding pair in their central chamber. There are even castes of workers of different sizes who perform separate tasks.

GLOSSARY

abdomen: the rear portion of an insect's body.

antennae: a pair of thin whip-like structures (feelers) on the head of an insect, which it uses to touch and smell.

aphid: any one of a number of soft-bodied insects that suck the juice from plants. Also called a plant louse.

brood cell: in the nest of a bee or wasp, a mud, wax or paper cell in which the young are reared.

caste: in any colony of social insects, a group of insects of distinctive size, shape and/or behavior which carry out special tasks. For example, soldier castes are specialized for guarding the nest and workers, while the queen's role is to lay eggs.

crop: a swollen chamber in the front part of the insect's gut in which it can store food.

excavate: to dig out.

fertilizing: adding the male insect's sperm to the female's eggs to make them grow.

forage: to go out and look for food.

gland: a special cluster of cells that produces a chemical for a specific purpose. For example, in honeybee workers some glands produce a special food for the larva, while others produce wax for building the nest.

larva (plural larvae): a young animal that hatches from an egg and looks very different from its parents.

molt: the shedding of the skin that occurs from time to time as an insect grows to allow it to get bigger.

nectar: the sweet sugary liquid found in the center of flowers.

nymph: a young insect that hatches from an egg and looks rather similar to its parents. Examples are the young of termites and grasshoppers.

pheromone: a special chemical produced in the body of an insect to send a specific message to other insects.

pollen: the powdery dust carried on the stamens of flowers. This is a good source of protein for growing insects. Actually, the pollen contains the flower's own sex cells, which need to reach the female parts of another flower to fertilize them.

pupa (plural pupae): the stage of an insect's life cycle in which the larva changes into the adult.

FURTHER READING

Baker, Wendy. *Insects*. New York: Thomson Learning, 1994.

Dorros, Arthur. *Ant Cities*. New York: Harper Collins Children's Books, 1987.

Chinery, Michael. How Bees Make Honey. Tarrytown, NY: Benchmark Books, 1997.

Fichter, George S. *Bees, Wasps, and Ants*. New York: Western Publishing, 1993.

Fischer-Nagel, Heiderose. *An Ant Colony*. Minneapolis, MN: Lerner, 1989.

Forsyth, Adrian. *Exploring the World of Insects: The Equinox Guide to Insect Behavior*. Buffalo, NY: Camden House, 1992.

Johnson, Sylvia A. *Wasps*. Minneapolis, MN: Lerner, 1984.

Julivert, Maria A. *The Fascinating World of Ants*. Hauppauge, NY: Barron's Educational Series, 1991.

Lavies, Bianca. *Killer Bees*. New York: Dutton Children's Books, 1994.

Oda, Hidemoto. *Insects and Their Homes*. Chatham, NJ: Raintree Steck-Vaughn, 1986.

Ogawa, Hiroshi. *The Potter Wasp*. Chatham, NJ: Raintree Steck-Vaughn, 1986.

Parramon, J.M. *The Fascinating World of Bees*. Hauppauge, NY: Barron's Educational Series, 1991.

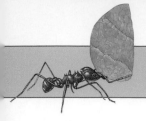

INDEX

Numbers in *italic* indicate pictures